Rosângela A. de Lima
Gleyciane M. da Silva
Marcela N. Ribeiro

Organisational climate and its influence on employee mental health

AF135558

Rosângela A. de Lima
Gleyciane M. da Silva
Marcela N. Ribeiro

Organisational climate and its influence on employee mental health

The importance of the Organisational Climate Diagnosis in the prevention of psychological pathologies

ScienciaScripts

Cover image: www.ingimage.com

This book is a translation from the original published under ISBN 978-613-9-77204-9.

Publisher:
Sciencia Scripts
is a trademark of
Dodo Books Indian Ocean Ltd. and OmniScriptum S.R.L publishing group

120 High Road, East Finchley, London, N2 9ED, United Kingdom
Str. Armeneasca 28/1, office 1, Chisinau MD-2012, Republic of Moldova, Europe
Printed at: see last page
ISBN: 978-620-6-53311-5

Summary:
The aim of this study was to carry out research into the diagnosis of the organisational climate at a large banking institution in the city of Goiânia, state of Goiás. The focus is on the influence of the organisational climate on employee mental health. It is based on the assumption that a harmonious organisational climate can improve productive capacity and can have a positive impact on employees' mental health.
bring benefits to workers' metal health. It is thus evident,
that psychological aspects are a determining factor in human performance. Therefore, a work team in a healthy environment tends to be more productive; it generates more efficient results; in short, it is decisive for the purposes of an organisation that wants to be profitable. The research was based on two studies, the results of which are presented in the discussion of the data. Study I used a semi-structured interview script with the managers and the content of the data collected was analysed according to Bardin (2002). In Study II, ECO (Organisational Climate Scale) questionnaires were used. The results indicate that the banking organisation needs interventions focused on motivational activities for staff and managers, training to guide the management of the workload and restructuring of the activities carried out at the banking organisation.

Keywords: Pathology; Mental Health; Overload.

Summary

Introduction

The *World Health Organisation* (2010) considers health, well-being and safety at work to be aspects of fundamental importance for the productivity, competitiveness and sustainability of organisations. Based on this concept, companies must consider the following factors: the costs of prevention *versus* the costs resulting from accidents and the financial consequences of ignoring labour laws and occupational health and safety standards (FARIA and VASCONCELOS, 2008, p.03).

The biggest challenge facing organisations today is to improve people management processes. And the "Organisational Climate" survey is seen as one of the most efficient diagnostic tools in the area of people management, considering that adherence to the principles of healthy working environments prevents absence from work and incapacity to work; minimises health costs; and minimises the costs associated with high turnover, thus increasing productivity (FARIA and VASCONCELOS, 2008, p.7-9). It is precisely this analysis that this work will be concerned with.

The specific objectives will focus on the importance of organisational diagnosis in order to propose interventions that make it possible to maintain a healthy organisational climate through practical procedures, such as applying questionnaires to analyse employees' perceptions of aspects associated with the work environment. Finally, to propose interventions that seek to remedy or reduce the weaknesses detected and consequently preserve workers' mental health.

The subject is justified for a number of reasons, including the need to theoretically investigate the fact that experience has shown that when workers are subjected to constant and intense levels of stress, aggravated by an overload of activities, their ability to carry out their tasks is compromised, interfering with the productivity of organisations.

The research method is descriptive and quantitative; exploratory and bibliographical, providing more data on the problem in order to give it greater clarity. The bibliographical research was carried out in works, scientific articles and indexed magazines that deal with the subject. Thus, the literature review provides the basis for what is proposed in the article. The exploratory research was based on interviews with permanent employees at a large banking institution. Finally, data collection and analysis will constitute the research procedure or methodology. The importance of this subject in the day-to-day running of organisations was noted, and the risks and benefits of this work were assessed in order to ensure the feasibility of carrying out the work.

The subject is undoubtedly relevant to the day-to-day running of organisations. In this way, the results of the research will contribute to the knowledge of the organisational climate found in the organisation, making it possible to identify which people management policies would be capable of dealing with the complexity of the human beings who work there; which organisational practices focusing on satisfaction, the development of competences, skills and a favourable organisational climate would be applicable to achieving the expected results: the preservation of workers' health.

CHAPTER 1

LITERATURE REVIEW

In order to understand the practice of the activities carried out in the field of study, we sought to analyse the theories and concepts inherent to the proposed theme.

Work is central to human life and is never neutral in relation to health (CARVALHO E MORAES, 2011). Suffering can be considered inseparable from both living and working. However, suffering can be a healthy option when creativity motivates individual subjectivity to access practical intelligence, co-operation and the dynamics of recognition. "In this process, work can be a mediator for health by strengthening identity" (CARVALHO and MORAES, 2011, p. 3).

Heloani and Capitão state that the balance of an individual's mental health is directly influenced by the work they do, because it is closely associated with personal fulfilment and the working conditions to which they are exposed (2003, p. 5).

According to the *World Health Organisation* (2002), working conditions (whether physical, chemical or biological) linked to their execution and organisation (structuring, hierarchy, division of tasks, working hours, pace, repetitiveness and excessive responsibility) can lead to workers becoming ill, as well as triggering psychological disorders (BENAGLIA, 2012, p. 3).

In addition to this, the *World Health Organisation has* provided general information on the health, safety and well-being of workers worldwide, recommending that risks be reduced in order to promote a healthier life in the workplace, in order to warn about the current situation that has worried thousands of professionals around the world (BENAGLIA, 2012, p. 5).

Based on this concept, it can be seen that adhering to the principles of environments favourable to worker wellbeing can prevent absenteeism, minimise health costs and the costs associated with high turnover, thus increasing productivity and, consequently, reflecting on the quality of products and services. And this proposed model consists of a process of continuous improvement based on ethics, values, top management engagement and worker

5

involvement.

Considering that companies are mainly made up of people, the attitude that provides the best chance of success lies in looking after your main source of productivity - your employees.

> While the company has its own needs, so do its employees. In order to reconcile the interests of both, a favourable organisational climate can contribute to this (OLIVEIRA, CARVALHO, ROSA, 2012, p. 02).

Chiavenato (1997) states that every organisation has an organisational climate, which is made up of its own psychological atmosphere and is related to morale and the satisfaction of what the members perceive as their needs, which can be: healthy or unhealthy, negative or positive, satisfactory or unsatisfactory, in other words, it will depend on the subject's perception of the company in which they are working.

According to Silva (2014), the Organisational Climate Diagnosis can be developed as an instrument that aims to quantitatively map, based on the perceptions of managers, workers and customers, the issues or problems that are perceived as essential and therefore need to be considered. "It is also a process of temporal and spatial verification in order to diagnose symptoms of inadequate procedures" (SILVA, 2014, p. 1).

Dorsch explains that the organisational diagnosis is built up through processes and is generally made up of stages:

> The initial or preliminary stage of contacting organisations has the exploratory purpose of gathering information. The initial purpose is to understand the problems pointed out by managers and other workers. These problems can be located in any area of the structure, processes and multiple, complex human interactions in organisations. Alternatives are then drawn up, followed by the construction of future scenarios, whose function is to generate proactivity by anticipating possible consequences. Action plans are then devised and put into practice, and finally the chosen actions are evaluated. The essential function of this stage is to feed back into the diagnostic process (*apud* SILVA, 2014, p. 1-2).

Considering the stages of the organisational climate diagnosis process described by Silva, we can see the importance of this tool for the process of changing work relations with a focus on workers' health. According to the same author, it is a tool that aids the process of both internal and external analysis of the organisation. And because it monitors employee satisfaction and commitment to the organisational guidelines, the diagnostic process makes it possible to develop strategic planning that produces actions that increase productivity and profitability, underpinned by a healthy working relationship between all employees in the organisation's hierarchical chain.

Carvalho and Moraes (2011) observed that the new forms of management related to the accumulation of capital have brought countless precariousness to labour relations, since they are based on constant threats of unemployment, supported by pressure and fierce competition. Thus, the new pathologies of labour proliferate, classified by Mendes (*apud* Carvalho and Moraes 2011, p.102-108) "as the pathology of overload, voluntary servitude and pressure for targets. In addition to these, there are signs and symptoms of stress, depression and anxiety that also constitute work-related illness". And this diagnosis can be verified when suffering at work is identified as a risk factor for illness.

Dejours (2005, p. 60-62) differentiates suffering into two types: (i) pathogenic suffering, which manifests itself when all possibilities for transformation, improvement and management are reached, and (ii) creative suffering, expressed in creative work actions. The latter enables the resignification of suffering and a positive structuring of identity, helping to strengthen subjective resistance to the various forms of psychic and bodily imbalances.

According to Heloani and Capitão (2003), short-term behaviour in today's working relationships has distorted the meaning of individual values. Employees are discarded by companies. On the other hand, employees no longer care about the meaning of their work or the opportunity to exchange experiences. The development of trust and mutual commitment have become obsolete values in the face of the desire to accumulate capital. It's as if everyone has become a market object. "True identification with work seems to live on in an objective that never materialises, since the actual work will only be momentary" (CAPITÃO and HELOANI, 2003, p. 6).

Freud (1987), when describing psychic development, reports that a newborn child does not yet differentiate its ego from the external world as the source of the countless sensations it experiences; only over time, and progressively, does it learn to make this differentiation,

7

reacting appropriately to the corresponding stimuli. According to Freud (1987), the ego, driven by the pleasure principle, tries to ward off unpleasant sensations, denoting a tendency to isolate and project outside itself everything that could be a source of displeasure and the ego can localise suffering from three directions: from our own body, from the external world and from our relationship with other people. These developments in the ego's avoidance of suffering can also occur in relation to work, from both a physical and mental point of view.

Thus, work becomes the representative of the force of the impulses that man employs to carry out a form of production that rules out the possibilities for the constitution of subjectivities. According to Heloani and Capitão (2003), by jeopardising the maintenance and strengthening of individual subjectivity, pathological work relationships annihilate the worker's psychic identity. Moral harassment, understood as a disciplinary process, exemplifies a type of pathological work relationship, considering that its practice seeks to depersonalise the identity of the harassed person through psychic weakening, thus constituting destabilising actions that compromise performance in work activities.

According to the same authors, when productivity excludes the subject, the following situations can occur:

> [...] dissemination of aggressive practices in relations between employees, generating indifference to the suffering of others and naturalisation of administrative excesses; little psychic disposition to face humiliation; fragmentation of affective ties; increase in individualism and establishment of the pact of collective silence; feeling of uselessness; lack of pleasure; forced resignation (HELOANI and CAPITÃO, 2003, p. 5).

Dejours (2005, p.133-139) states that "[...] the depressive experience in relation to work and oneself is fed by the sensation of intellectual numbness, mental sclerosis, paralysis of fantasy and imagination [...]"; in other words, when the standardisation of worker conditioning is sought to the detriment of productive and creative behaviour, subjectivity is annihilated, causing mental fatigue that causes "psychic pain".

Complementing this concept,

> work can produce insurmountable suffering for the ego, impoverishing it and restricting its action to repetitive and ineffective defensive mechanisms, preventing it from discerning, according to its activities, the satisfaction of certain drives. And this situation of suffering generates anguish, depressive states, anxiety, non-specific fears, somatic symptoms, as marked signs of

8

mental suffering, with the aggravating factor that a weakened and fragile ego is unable to differentiate the origin of its suffering (CAPITÃO and HELOANI, 2003, p. 6).

According to Jacques (2007), this will provide psychologists and other mental health professionals with a huge field of study, not just denunciation. When employees are motivated, they cause major and profound changes in the company they work for, as they will propose strategies to improve the working environment and thus provide an environment that allows other employees to continue and carry out their work with dedication and motivation. When there are changes at this level in a company, not only will the employee reach the highest level of Maslow's pyramid, which is self-actualisation, but both they and the company will be satisfied with the results and the increase in demand and profitability.

The psychodynamics of work is a theoretical and methodological approach based on the principles of psychoanalysis and the social sciences in labour relations:

> Work Psychodynamics has a methodological focus on the collective issues of workers, considering their subjective aspects by analysing their experiences of pleasure and suffering, their coping strategies and the senses and meanings implicit in the individual-work relationship (FLEURY and MACÊDO, 2015, p. 95).

The pressures of work and mental illness get in the way, preventing an individual from reacting and defending themselves, especially if they are part of a community that develops a defensive ideology, capable of masking their reality and making the unbearable bearable (FLEURY and MACÊDO, 2015, p. 95).

When the labour clinic bases its practice on a psychodynamic approach to work, then it applies a comprehensive analysis of the pleasure-suffering dynamic in the work context in order to prevent illness (FLEURY and MACÊDO, 2015, p.96).

However, although suffering is present in work situations, it is denied by political and trade union organisations with the aim of concealing reality and promoting behaviours that are increasingly committed to organisational challenges. And through this constructed reality, organisations look to workers' suffering for elements to increase productivity (FLEURY and MACÊDO, 2015, p.103).

According to Fleury and Macêdo,

9

workers' suffering is exploited in order to increase the production system. To achieve this, companies encourage the vicious circle between nervous tension and productivity to continue. This process takes place in such a way that the more tense, aggressive, anxious and fearful workers are, the more productive they become (2015, p. 104).

Complementing the concepts set out by Fleury and Macêdo, Landim, Bezerra, Alves and Marx (2017, p.189) state that:

> The health-disease process should not be analysed outside the context in which it takes place. Therefore, it cannot be analysed to the exclusion of the subject who suffers. Work is a central support for maintaining life and for the meaning of the self in the collective. [...] Illness from work, as well as the ability to overcome the limits of illness, depend on a socially constructed relationship between the subject and work, in a very particular and individualised way.

It can be said that there are stressful places to work. However, these contingencies cannot be a reason for individuals to stop playing their role in the company. Individuals need to use their creativity to transform the work environment and this will only happen if they have a reason to change the reality around them.

Therefore, based on the quotes described, the following understanding is possible: pleasure and suffering originate from an internal dynamic. And in work relationships, they are the result of the attitudes and behaviours of the organisational design, whose background is made up of subjective and power relations. Due to the established condition of mental functioning, the subject loses their autonomy and their ego is weakened, they don't have the strength to carry out the work in which their entire existence is involved. And when there is a blockage between the relationship between man and the meaningful content of work, pathological suffering occurs and consequently the employee becomes ill, jeopardising both their health and the company's productivity and profitability.

CHAPTER 2

METHODOLOGY

The study used exploratory, descriptive, quantitative and bibliographical research. The population, the object of study and data collection, is made up of permanent employees at a large banking institution located in the city of Goiânia, in the state of Goiás. Random samples were used from among the organisation's leaders and representative of the employees, considering the subject matter and the company's demands.

The exploratory research was carried out in March and April 2016. Firstly, a semi-structured interview script drawn up by Professor Alessandra Ramos Demito Fleury (2016) was used. Four (4) employees in leadership positions took part in the semi-structured interview. However, a total of 13 (thirteen) managers were invited. The second stage used the ECO questionnaire - *Organisational Climate Scale,* taken from the book *Measures of Organisational Behaviour,* by Maria do Carmo Fernandes Martins (2008). Twenty (20) employees took part in this data collection, from a universe of seventy (70) employees. The (i) "inclusion criteria" were bank employees working in a branch in the city of Goiânia, of both sexes; and the (ii) "exclusion criteria" were bank employees who had already acquired the right to retire and employees with a self-reported psychiatric diagnosis.

The data collected through the semi-structured interview was analysed using Bardin's (2002) content analysis and Windows Excel® software was used for the information collected through the ECO questionnaire. The results were presented separately and related in the discussion of the data.

The data collected, which formed the basis for the analysis of the Organisational Diagnosis at the bank under study, was obtained with the utmost care for ethics, and the employees, managers and the institution itself opted for total anonymity.

CHAPTER 3

RESULTS AND DISCUSSION

Analysing the data collected showed a gender balance between female (58.33%) and male (41.67%) employees, which led to the conclusion that women have equal opportunities in the company. Analysing the information collected, it can also be seen that the majority of employees (83.33%), 20 out of a total of 24, work 6-hour days, while (16.67%), out of a total of 24, work 8-hour days. It should be emphasised that the workers who work longer hours are those in management and supervisory positions.

The analysis of employees' perceptions of the Organisation under study was based on the five factors that make up the *ECO Scale*.

> The ECO is a multidimensional scale built and validated with the aim of assessing workers' perceptions of various dimensions of the organisational climate. The responses of the participating workers were subjected to principal axis analysis with oblique (Oblimin) and orthogonal (Varimax) rotations, the former to test for intercorrelations between factors and the latter to extract them. Factors with eigenvalues greater than or equal to 1.5 that explained at least 2 per cent of the total variance each and items with factor loadings greater than or equal to 0.40 remained in the Scale. The final validated Scale was made up of sixty-three items grouped into five factors that explained 35% of the total variance, all semantically interpretable, called Support from management and organisation (**Factor I**, with 21 items and a precision index of 0.92); Reward (Factor **II**, with 13 items and a precision index of 0.88); Physical Comfort (Factor **III**, with 13 items and a precision index of 0.86); Control and Pressure (Factor **IV**, with 9 items and a precision index of 0.78) and Cohesion between colleagues (Factor **V**, with 7 items and a precision index of 0.78) (SIQUEIRA, 2008, p. 34 - 78). 34 - 36).

Complementing the information on the *ECO Scale*, Piovezan and Rubino (2011, p. 30) state that the averages obtained through the *ECO Scale* should be interpreted:

> [...] consider that the higher the factor mean, the better the organisational climate, i.e. values greater than 4 tend to indicate a good climate and values less than 2.9 indicate a bad climate. However, for Factor 4 (control/pressure) it's the other way round, in which case the higher the score, the worse the climate because the greater the control and pressure exerted on employees. It is also important to emphasise that the ECO is a scale resulting from a long empirical study that has demonstrated its validity and reliability [...]

In order to find a more precise and effective diagnosis, the organisation under study was analysed in four different areas: (i) "Individual Service"; (ii) "Individual Service

Support"; (iii) "Cashier Service" and (iv) "Housing Service/Support". The ECO was applied in each area at different times. The results were presented based on the average obtained for each factor.

The appendices show the results as well as the most compromised items in each Scale Factor per area analysed.

3.1 Factor I of the *ECO Scale*: Support from management and the organisation

According to Siqueira (2008), in the *ECO Scale*, Factor I ("Support from management and the organisation") measures the affective, structural and operational support from management and the organisation provided to employees in the daily performance of their work activities. And this Factor for the Individual Customer Service Area pointed to two negative items, no positive items, an average of 3.0 indicating a "Regular Climate". It was found that the data collected anonymously and the data collected in interviews with managers differed in the perception of employees on the issue of authority. The scores on the *ECO Scale* show a perception of commitment on Factor I, and the verbalisations of the managers in the interview showed discomfort denounced by their body language. For this analysis, we also looked at the Psychophysiological Principle formulated by Greenne in 1970, according to Weil and Tompakow (2009, p. 169):

> Every change in the physiological state is accompanied by an appropriate change in the mental-emotional state; and reciprocally every change in the metal-emotional state is accompanied by an appropriate change in the physiological state.

Based on this analysis, the perception of employees and managers was that Factor I can interfere with intrapersonal relationships and, consequently, motivation.

According to Souza (2009), when a worker is promoted to a management position, he will have to deal not only with targets and performance, but also with the feelings of weakness of each member of his team. They will have to exercise leadership in pursuit of the best results. It is therefore essential to prepare managers to deal with new issues and, above all, with the emotions of their team members. And it's up to the company to provide this training even before the promotion takes place (SOUZA, 2009, p.184).

3.2 Factor II of the *ECO Scale*: Reward

According to Siqueira (2008), Factor II (Reward) of the *ECO Scale* assesses the numerous forms of rewards that companies use to recognise employees' work in terms of quality, productivity, effort and performance. This factor implies the re-signification of suffering at work, and as such deserves attention.

Factor II was found to be compromised in all areas. Workers' perception of the lack of recognition for their productivity. For employees in the "Personal Service Area", Factor II indicated four negative items, with the item "rewards for worker productivity" being the most compromised; no positive items and an average of 2.7 indicating a "negative climate". For employees in the "Support for Individual Customer Service" area, Factor II indicated one negative item, with "rewards for productivity" being the most compromised, no positive items and an average of 2.7, indicating a "negative climate". Factor II pointed to four negative items for employees in the "Cashier Service" area, with the "reward for productivity" item being the most compromised, no positive items and an average of 2.7, indicating a "negative climate". As for employees in the "Customer Service/Housing Support" area, Factor II indicated one negative item, with the "reward for productivity" item being the most compromised, no positive items and an average of 3.2 indicating a "regular climate".

According to Harter and Wagner,

> Neuroscientists believe that the ventral striatum and nucleus accumbens together form a basic reward processing centre and that a neurotransmitter called dopamine activates it, providing a sense of pleasure and satisfaction. And it turned out that positive words specifically activate regions of the brain linked to reward. One employee interviewed by Gallup World Poll tried to put the effect into words: "For me, receiving praise and recognition seems to trigger a little internal explosion. It gives you a feeling of, 'Oh, that was good, but you know what? I can do better'. It gives us an incentive to keep trying, to become even better" (HARTER and WAGNER, 2009, p.87-88).

According to Harter and Wagner (*ibid.*), if an employee expects to be recognised for their work, the disappointment of receiving only silence causes a drop in their dopamine levels. And the drop in the neurotransmitter conditions the employee to avoid a "thankless" task, i.e. if the task needs to be done in order for the employee to get paid, they will probably reduce the effort to the minimum necessary, thus generating a demotivational factor.

14

Complementing the concept of Harter and Wagner (2009), Mendes states that pleasure in the context of work happens when you experience gratification and freedom.

> Gratification is the feeling of satisfaction, fulfilment, pride and identification with a job that meets professional aspirations. Freedom is the feeling of being free to think, organise and talk about work, considering that the particular way of working is recognised by managers and colleagues (MENDES, 2004, p. 155-156).

For this author, the experiences of pleasure-suffering form a single construct, made up of four factors: gratification, freedom, insecurity and wear and tear (*ibidem*).

3.3 Factor III of the *ECO Scale*: Physical Comfort

According to Siqueira (2008), Factor III (Physical Comfort) of the *ECO Scale* assesses the physical environment, safety and comfort provided by the company to employees. The perception of employees in the "Personal Service" area pointed to two negative items for Factor II, with the item "airy workplace" being the most compromised; one positive item (clean workplace) and an average of 3.0 indicating a "regular climate". For employees in the "Support for Individual Customer Service" area, Factor III indicated one negative item, with "insufficient physical space" being the most compromised; one positive item "clean workplace", and an average of 3.4 indicating a "regular climate". For employees in the "Cashier Service" area, Factor III indicated four negative items, with the item "adequate physical space to guarantee employee health" being the most compromised, no positive items and an average of 3.1 indicating a "regular climate". For employees in the "Customer Service/Housing Support" area, Factor III indicated one negative item, with the item "airy physical space" being the most compromised, no positive items and an average of 3.6 indicating a "regular climate".

It is important to emphasise the importance of physical ergonomics in the performance of workers' activities. The *International Ergonomics Association* (IEA) (2012) (*apud* JUNIOR, SILVA, SILVA and NASCIMENTO, 2013) describes the environmental aspects (physical - noise, lighting, temperature) needed to ensure worker health:

> A sound sensation is perceived as noise when it is annoying or unwanted. The negative effects of noise can cause physiological problems that can lead to

15

permanent hearing damage.

Lighting must be evenly distributed to avoid glare, annoying reflections, shadows and excessive contrasts. And visual comfort is adequate accommodation, defined as the ability to focus on objects at different distances, which allows the sharpest focus of the object on the retina, and in this case, lighting is decisive.

And thermal comfort is an essential condition for health, safety and productivity, because humans are homeothermic animals, who keep their bodies at approximately 37°C regardless of the external temperature, maintained by a physiological control system of thermal balance. (JUNIOR, SILVA, SILVA, NASCIMENTO, 2013, p.03).

Also according to the authors, ergonomic data (excessive force, high repetitiveness, incorrect postures, among others) are considered to be the main factors responsible for workers becoming ill in organisations.

The whole act of carrying out a task, according to Junior, Silva, Silva and Nascimento (*ibidem*), can be tedious for the worker and can cause some health problems. In this sense, in order to mitigate the possible risks of occurrences caused by inadequate work space, ergonomics is a science that studies the suitability of work for human beings.

Organisations therefore generate dysfunctions in adapting work to people, and because of this it is necessary to use ergonomic analyses to improve the suitability of the working environment.

3.4 Factor IV of the *ECO Scale*: Control and Pressure

According to Siqueira (2008), Factor IV (Control and Pressure) of the *ECO Scale* assesses the control and pressure exerted by the company and supervisors on employee behaviour and performance. Employees in the "Individual Customer Service" area rated Factor IV highly negatively (4.0), with no positive items and an average of 2.7, indicating a "regular climate". Employees in the "Individual Customer Service Support" area had a high negative score for Factor IV (4.0), with the item "Organisation's demand for punctuality in the delivery of tasks" being the most compromised; two positive items on the "exaggerated control" question; and an average score of 3.2, indicating a "Regular Climate". Employees in the "Cashier Service" area had a high negative score for Factor IV (4.0), with the item "Organisation's demand for punctuality in the delivery of tasks" being the most compromised;

no positive items and an average of 3.3, indicating a "regular climate". Employees in the "Customer Service/Housing Support" area rated Factor IV highly negatively (4.0), with the item "Organisation's demand for punctuality in the delivery of tasks" being the most compromised; two positive items on the "exaggerated control" question; and an average of 3.0 indicating a "regular climate".

In the questionnaires answered anonymously (items 44 to 52 of the *ECO Scale*), the majority of workers perceived the presence of a controlling manager. And the interviews with managers revealed a possible rigid administrative policy in the organisation. This factor shows that workers are uncomfortable expressing their opinions about management, perhaps for fear of retaliation.

Dejours (2005, p. 119-131) points out that

> [...] the fragility of the spirit of co-operation, the denial of suffering resulting from work, the discrepancy between what is prescribed and what is real, associated with the predominance of rigid controls, are all factors that trigger pathological suffering at work.

Agreeing with this idea, Moraes and Carvalho (2011, p. 1-10) point out that organisational factors where pressure is evident (be it for targets or an accelerated pace of work by the boss) as well as the collective strategy of self-acceleration promote and enhance, even if indirectly, illness in work relationships.

According to Moraes and Carvalho (*ibidem*), work overload, pressure for results and the fear of losing one's job establish a pathogenic work rhythm. The focus on achieving excellence in results reinforces the pathology of work overload that exceeds the limits of human conditions. And this pathology, in turn, highlights the alienation of individual desire, which sees the organisation's goals as its own, and these, once achieved, are raised incessantly, aggravating the excessive workload and leading to illness.

Dejours (2005, p. 126-132) highlights as evidence of the pathology of overload the rapid increase in mental decompensation or somatic illnesses, among other pathological conditions such as *karoshi* (sudden death due to exhaustion at work).

For Mendes and Resende,

> When there is no room for the expression of individuality, when there is no

17

recognition, when the system is rigid in a way that doesn't allow workers to mobilise, they resort to defence mechanisms, which are characterised by behaviours of psycho-affective and professional isolation from the work group, resignation, disbelief, renunciation of participation, indifference and apathy. These defences play an ambiguous role: while on the one hand they are necessary to maintain psychic equilibrium, on the other they can lead to immobility and alienation. And this defensive strategy, of rationalisation and competitive individualism, is faced with the high prevalence of illnesses, but mainly attributes to the fear of exclusion the factor that would justify the fact that workers endure the current working conditions in banks (2004, p.151-172).

Work, in any circumstance, always produces some wear and tear and nowadays, according to Bock, Furtado and Teixeira (2012), the worker, in addition to their body, must involve their subjectivity in the production process. And part of this tension is transformed into subjective wear and tear. And a working climate that enhances subjective relationships creates new forms of relationship. Because before, bosses demanded an increase in production and now they want greater involvement, greater commitment and a more proactive attitude. And this pressure can turn into undue pressure.

The authoritarian climate and its implications for organisations have been revealed in the intense discussions about bullying. And bullying can make its victims ill, and the worker may suffer from insomnia, gastritis, hypertension, anxiety, depression and even more serious cases such as *Burnout Syndrome* (emotional exhaustion related to work, causing the worker to be dissatisfied, exhausted and totally lacking in motivation - BOCK, FURTADO e TEIXEIRA, 2012, p.37-38; 169).

Chiavenato (1997, p. 53) believes that motivating the employee

> Internal forces within the individual reinforce persistence in dedication to work; and this internal state can result from a need. Motivation is described as an activator or arouser of behaviour generally directed towards satisfying a need; factors that provoke, channel and sustain behaviour.

According to the same author, organisations need to be careful when setting their objectives, because if they are easily achievable, they won't mobilise people and, on the other hand, if they are blocked or prevented from achieving an objective, people will become frustrated. And productivity is the relationship between the products obtained and the factors of production used to obtain them.

Complementing Chiavenato's (1997) ideas, Robbins apud Souza (2010) states that

18

when we join an organisation, we bring our values with us and this will influence the way we see and deal with situations. And our attitudes are directly related to our values. And people seek consistency in their attitudes and behaviour. (SOUZA, 2010)

These concepts can be summarised using the ideas put forward by Bock, Furtado and Teixeira (2012):

> In everyday life, people have needs and feel a lack of something. A need is a psychological state that sets people in motion to look for what object in the world around us might seem satisfactory to solve the need. On finding this object, we can say that the subject now has a motive: a relationship between a need and a goal. The willingness to set in motion (behaviour) in the direction of obtaining the object is what we call motivation (BOCK, FURTANDO, TEIXEIRA, 2012, p.121).

3.5 Factor V of the *ECO Scale*: Cohesion between colleagues

According to Siqueira (2008), Factor V (Cohesion between colleagues) in the *ECO Scale* assesses unity, bonds and collaboration between co-workers. The perception of employees in the "Individual Customer Service" area pointed to no negative items and no positive items for Factor V, an average of 3.4, indicating a "regular climate". And with the data collection, both in the observational activities and through the data collected in the *ECO Scale* and in the semi-structured interview with the managers, it was found that despite the overload of activities, the intrapersonal relationship appears regular and socialising is perceived as pleasurable. Employees in the "Customer Service/Housing Support" area reported no negative items for Factor V, two positive items for "friendship and companionship" and an average of 3.6 indicating a "regular climate".

According to Mendes, the psychodynamics of work means that the experiences of pleasure-suffering are part of an intersubjective relationship and occur mainly as a result of the organisation of work, in issues directly linked to the work activity itself, and also to socio-professional relationships with the company, the boss and work colleagues (MENDES, 2004, p. 151-175).

In agreement with Mendes, Harter and Wagner state that the workplace has a special importance for most employees in a society that has lost much of the social contact of previous generations.

For decades, sociologists have observed a decline in people joining clubs, attending parent-teacher meetings at schools, attending municipal meetings, joining political parties, going to church or cultivating social ties, such as going to dinner at the neighbour's house. Each generation has a lower level of trust in those around them than the previous generation. One of the most disturbing findings was that between 1985 and 2004, the average person's circle of friends fell from around three to two friends and the number of people who say they have no one to discuss important matters with almost tripled (HARTER, WAGNER, 2009, p.196).

According to these authors, half a century of cultural change has made the world outside work less friendly and sociable and the workplace, once a place for social interaction, is now becoming relatively exceptional. For both self-employed professionals and industrial workers are spending many hours together. So for many lonely people, work has become home.

But it is important to emphasise that, according to the same authors, friendship is not without risks for productivity, nor is it effective without other elements, such as the commitment of colleagues to quality work or clear expectations for each team member. Without a clear direction, very cohesive teams can get lost in social interactions and ignore the needs of clients or the company. A group needs norms as well as cohesion.

Finally, the best managers encourage friendships in the workplace, creating the conditions for them to "sprout", because most of the data indicates that the closer the group is, the better it performs on a routine basis, even when subjected to a load of pressure (HARTER and WAGNER, 2009, p. 200-201).

After analysing the data collected, both through the semi-structured interview with managers and the *ECO Scale* questionnaire with employees, it emerged that in the perception of workers, the overall average of the institution varies from fair to negative, pointing to the need for intervention in order to prevent employees from becoming ill.

It is also important to emphasise that among the most aggravated factors, Factors II (Rewards) and IV (Control/pressure) are the most worrying, because according to Junior, Silva, Silva and Nascimento (2013, p. 4):

Ergonomic analysis of cognitive work seeks to demonstrate situations in which the subject receives or exchanges more information than they can handle, and can make mistakes with this excess of information. Cognitive assessment studies direct the company towards analysing indicators of the degree of mental fatigue or stress and the extent to which this will determine the productivity and quality of life of employees.

According to the same authors (*ibid.*), factors that compromise both physical and organisational ergonomics (concentration of movements in the same person, overtime, double shifts, a tight work schedule, lack of breaks) and cognitive ergonomics (excessive pressure for results, a tense environment, interpersonal relationship problems, lack of pleasure, lack of recognition for work) are the main causes of illness in organisations.

Reinforcing this concept, Rodrigues and Mollica state that

> the pressure to meet targets is one of the main causes of illness, both through repetitive effort and mental exhaustion. The system of meeting targets (especially for sales of financial products to customers) appears as a major villain among the sources of stress and illness (2016, p. 44).

Complementing the position of the aforementioned authors, Evangelista (2010, p.11) states that rewards motivate employees and can be tangible, such as a cash bonus, or intangible, such as praise. And the convergence between individual and organisational values contributes to the formation of favourable perceptions of business dynamics, with repercussions on performance and involvement at work.

Based on these quotes, we can conclude with the understanding that pleasure and suffering originate from self-knowledge. And work relationships are the result of attitudes and behaviours defined by the organisational culture. When workers lose their autonomy, their subjectivity is violated and they become vulnerable to psychic imbalances, weakening their chances of carrying out the work in which their entire existence is involved. And when there is a blockage between man's relationship with the meaningful content of work, pathological suffering occurs and consequently the employee becomes ill, jeopardising both their health and the company's productivity and profitability.

CHAPTER 4

FINAL CONSIDERATIONS

It is well known that the banking sector is a segment of the labour market that has been undergoing significant transformations and this reality accentuates the physical and mental demands on workers.

Based on the analysis of the data obtained through observational activities, semi-structured interviews and the application of the *ECO Scale,* carried out at the bank that is the object of this article's study, the need for training with leaders and motivational activities with employees was observed.

In order to practice motivational activities, knowledge of human resources management is essential in order to recognise and value the subjectivity of each team member, since the introjection of motivated behaviour is achieved through individual satisfaction.

From studying the articles and concepts of thinkers such as Dejours, Chiavenato and others, it can be seen that organisations need to be careful when setting their objectives. Goals set in an unattainable reality, aimed solely at profit, will not mobilise employees; on the other hand, failure to achieve a goal is a factor that increases feelings of frustration. And productivity, which is the relationship between the products obtained and the factors of production used to obtain them, is compromised in both quantity and quality.

It is also understood that subjective values influence the way we see and understand the situations that make up a reality. And each attitude is directly related to individual values. People need subjective confirmation for their attitudes and behaviour in order to reinforce the goal of every being, which is to feel their existence and not just to exist.

In order to apply training to leaders, it is essential to understand the difference between training and people development. While training is focussed on the current position, seeking to improve the skills required for the immediate performance of the position, people development is aimed at the positions to be filled in the future and the new skills that will be required (VOLPE, 2009).

22

According to the same author, for large organisations, training is not just seen as an expense, but as an investment practice for both the organisation and its employees, which is why training and developing people has become increasingly present in the activities of organisations because it is capable of enriching the company's human assets and is also responsible for the intellectual capital of organisations (VOLPE, 2009, p. 1).

Thus, based on the scientific evidence that underpins this article, there was a need to present intervention proposals in order to meet the needs identified in the data collected from the institution under study.

Considering the commitment of factor I (managerial/organisational support), it was proposed that managers add *feedback to* their teams' routines, based on the diagnosis of the feeling of repression perceived by the majority of employees, which can lead to a demotivational factor in the team. It is important to emphasise that it is essential to have a private environment in which to give *feedback so that* employees feel comfortable expressing their opinions. It was also found that the ll factor (reward) scored below average, according to the perception of the majority of employees. This item is worrying because it directly affects employees' mental health.

It was therefore proposed that employees be recognised for their efforts in routine activities and not just in activities focused on achieving sales campaign targets. Another item that gave cause for concern was Factor IV (control and pressure). In the perception of the majority of employees, there is a constant routine of controlling activities, both in terms of deadlines and the number of activities carried out each day. This item exposes the diagnosis of activity overload, another element that considerably compromises the employee's health, not only physically, but mainly mentally, as the worker carries out their activities in a situation of constant and intense stress.

It can therefore be said that a motivated employee is able to carry out their activities with satisfaction and efficiency, increasing their chances of growth and, at the same time, the organisation will have a greater chance of success by gaining a foothold in the market. The result is the profit achieved by the organisation through the targets set without, however, disrespecting the subjectivity of each team member, thus safeguarding the employee's metal health.

CHAPTER 5

Appendices

Appendix I

Organisational Climate Scale - ECO

In this questionnaire you'll find a series of phrases that describe company characteristics and that have been collected from different work organisations.
Please rate how well these characteristics describe the company where you work. The important thing is that you give your opinion on the characteristics of your company as a whole.
To answer, read the characteristics described in the sentences and tick next to each sentence the number that best represents your opinion, according to the following scale:

	1	2	3	4	5
01. My sector is informed of decisions involving it.	Strongly disagree	I disagree	Neither agree nor disagree	I agree	I totally agree
02. The conflicts that occur in my work are resolved by the group itself.	Strongly disagree	I disagree	Neither agree nor disagree	I agree	I totally agree
03. The employee receives guidance from the supervisor (or boss) to carry out their tasks.	Strongly disagree	I disagree	Neither agree nor disagree	I agree	I totally agree
04. Tasks that take longer to complete are guided to the end by the boss.	Strongly disagree	I disagree	Neither agree nor disagree	I agree	I totally agree
05. Here, the boss helps employees with problems.	Strongly disagree	I disagree	Neither agree nor disagree	I agree	I totally agree
06. The boss praises when the employee does a good job.	Strongly disagree	I disagree	Neither agree nor disagree	I agree	I totally agree
07. The changes are monitored by supervisors (or bosses).	Strongly disagree	I disagree	Neither agree nor disagree	I agree	I totally agree
08. Employees are informed of changes in the company.	Strongly disagree	I disagree	Neither agree nor disagree	I agree	I totally agree
09. In this company, doubts are cleared up.	Strongly disagree	I disagree	Neither agree nor disagree	I agree	I totally agree
10. There is task planning here.	Strongly disagree	I disagree	I neither agree nor disagree	I agree	I totally agree
11. The employee can count on the support of the boss	Strongly disagree	I disagree	Neither agree nor disagree	I agree	I totally agree
12. Changes in this company are planned.	Strongly disagree	I disagree	Neither agree nor disagree	I agree	I totally agree
13. Innovations made by employees in their work are accepted by the company.	Strongly disagree	I disagree	Neither agree nor disagree	I agree	I totally agree

			Neither		
14. Here, new ideas improve employee performance.	Strongly disagree	I disagree	Neither agree nor disagree	I agree	I totally agree
15. The boss values the employee's opinion.	Strongly disagree	I disagree	Neither agree nor disagree	I agree	I totally agree
16. In this company, employees have a say in changes.	Strongly disagree	I disagree	Neither agree nor disagree	I agree	I totally agree
17. The boss has respect for the employee.	Strongly disagree	I disagree	Neither agree nor disagree	I agree	I totally agree
18. The boss collaborates with employee productivity.	Strongly disagree	I disagree	Neither agree nor disagree	I agree	I totally agree
19. In this company, the boss helps the employee when he needs it.	Strongly disagree	I disagree	Neither agree nor disagree	I agree	I totally agree
20. The company accepts new ways for employees to carry out their tasks.	Strongly disagree	I disagree	Neither agree nor disagree	I agree	I totally agree
21. Dialogue is used to solve the company's problems.	Strongly disagree	I disagree	Neither agree nor disagree	I agree	I totally agree
22. Employees carry out their tasks with satisfaction.	Strongly disagree	I disagree	Neither agree nor disagree	I agree	I totally agree
23. Here, the boss values his employees.	Strongly disagree	I disagree	Neither agree nor disagree	I agree	I totally agree
24. When employees do their job well, they are rewarded.	Strongly disagree	I disagree	Neither agree nor disagree	I agree	I totally agree
25. What employees earn depends on the tasks they do.	Strongly disagree	I disagree	Neither agree nor disagree	I agree	I totally agree
26. In this company, employees know why they are being rewarded.	Strongly disagree	I disagree	Neither agree nor disagree	I agree	I totally agree
27. This company cares about the health of its employees.	Strongly disagree	I disagree	Neither agree nor disagree	I agree	I totally agree
28. This company values employee effort.	Strongly disagree	I disagree	Neither agree nor disagree	I agree	I totally agree
29. The rewards the employee receives are within their expectations.	Strongly disagree	I disagree	Neither agree nor disagree	I agree	I totally agree
30. A job well done is rewarded.	Strongly disagree	I disagree	Neither agree nor disagree	I agree	I totally agree
31. The employees of this company have the necessary equipment to carry out their tasks.	Strongly disagree	I disagree	Neither agree nor disagree	I agree	I totally agree
32. The working environment meets the physical needs of the worker.	Strongly disagree	I disagree	Neither agree nor disagree	I agree	I totally agree
33. In this company, the disabled can move around easily.	Strongly disagree	I disagree	Neither agree nor disagree	I agree	I totally agree
34. The physical space in the work area is sufficient.	Strongly disagree	I disagree	Neither agree nor	I agree	I totally agree

			disagree		
35. The physical working environment is pleasant.	Strongly disagree	I disagree	Neither agree nor disagree	I agree	I totally agree
36. In this company, the workplace is airy.	Strongly disagree	I disagree	Neither agree nor disagree	I agree	I totally agree
37. In this company, there is equipment to prevent hazards at work.	Strongly disagree	I disagree	Neither agree nor disagree	I agree	I totally agree
38. There is adequate lighting in the workplace.	Strongly disagree	I disagree	Neither agree nor disagree	I agree	I totally agree
39. This company shows concern for safety at work.	Strongly disagree	I disagree	Neither agree nor disagree	I agree	I totally agree
40. The work area is clean.	Strongly disagree	I disagree	Neither agree nor disagree	I agree	I totally agree
41. Work equipment is adequate to guarantee employee health at work.	Strongly disagree	I disagree	Neither agree nor disagree	I agree	I totally agree
42. In this company, the physical posture of the employees is adequate to avoid damaging their health.	Strongly disagree	I disagree	Neither agree nor disagree	I agree	I totally agree
43. The work environment facilitates the performance of tasks.	Strongly disagree	I disagree	Neither agree nor disagree	I agree	I totally agree
44. There is too much control over employees here.	Strongly disagree	I disagree	Neither agree nor disagree	I agree	I totally agree
45. In this company, everything is controlled.	Strongly disagree	I disagree	Neither agree nor disagree	I agree	I totally agree
46. This company demands that tasks be done on time.	Strongly disagree	I disagree	Neither agree nor disagree	I agree	I totally agree
47. Employee attendance is strictly controlled by the company.	Strongly disagree	I disagree	Neither agree nor disagree	I agree	I totally agree
48. Here, the boss uses company rules to punish employees.	Strongly disagree	I disagree	Neither agree nor disagree	I agree	I totally agree
49. Staff hours are strictly enforced.	Strongly disagree	I disagree	Neither agree nor disagree	I agree	I totally agree
50. Here, the boss presses all the time.	Strongly disagree	I disagree	Neither agree nor disagree	I agree	I totally agree
51. In this company, nothing is done without the boss's authorisation.	Strongly disagree	I disagree	Neither agree nor disagree	I agree	I totally agree
52. In this company there is permanent supervision by the boss.	Strongly disagree	I disagree	Neither agree nor disagree	I agree	I totally agree
53. Relationships between people in this sector are friendly.	Strongly disagree	I disagree	Neither agree nor disagree	I agree	I totally agree
54. Employees who make a mistake are helped by their colleagues.	Strongly disagree	I disagree	Neither agree nor disagree	I agree	I totally agree
55. Here, colleagues help a new employee	Strongly	I disagree	Neither	I agree	I totally

with their difficulties.	disagree		agree nor disagree		agree
56. There is co-operation between colleagues in this company.	Strongly disagree	I disagree	Neither agree nor disagree	I agree	I totally agree
57. In this company, employees welcome a new colleague.	Strongly disagree	I disagree	Neither agree nor disagree	I agree	I totally agree
58. There is integration between colleagues and employees in this company.	Strongly disagree	I disagree	Neither agree nor disagree	I agree	I totally agree
59. Employees feel comfortable telling some of their colleagues about their personal problems.					

Appendix II

Script for semi-structured interviews with leaders Author: Alessandra Ramos Demito Fleury

1. Rapport and presentation of the agreement and the research objectives.

2. A brief account of the employee's history with the company.

3. Every organisation has ethical principles that guide the actions of those who make it up. For the principles to form the **values of** an organisation, they have to be authentic and experienced by everyone. For example, transparency, ethics..., which symbolise the actions of all those who are part of the organisation. What are the main values that employees share in their work?
   1°.-
   2°-
   3°-

4. How would you rate the company's image among the population of Goiânia?

BadBadRegularGood	Excellent
1234	5

5. What other companies would be considered "competitors" of _____ ?
6. How do you rate its performance in _____ relation to them?

Strengths

7. In your opinion, what are the company's main strengths? A **strength** is something the organisation does well or a characteristic that gives it an important capability that contributes to its success. Try to name the 3 main ones:

Weak points

8. A **weakness** is something that the organisation doesn't have or doesn't do very well and that compromises the company's success. Try to highlight, in your opinion, the company's main weaknesses (try to name at least the top 3):

10. What kind of company training could bring improvements?

11. What additional **suggestions, comments, compliments or criticisms** would you make of the company ___ ?

Annexes

Annex I

Script for semi-structured interviews with leaders
Author: Professor Alessandra Ramos Demito Fleury

Question 1: Every organisation has ethical principles that guide the actions of *its* members. For the principles to form the values of an organisation, they must be authentic and experienced by everyone. For example, transparency, ethics..., which symbolise the actions of all those who are part of the organisation. What are the main values that employees share in their work?

Category	Frequency	Verbalisation
Ethics	3	PI "Ethics, companionship and dedication..." PI sighed and thought for a moment before answering.
Commitment	3	P4 "Commitment, interpersonal relationships and loyalty" P4 scratches his head and crosses his arms.
Companionship	2	P2 "Commitment, ethics and companionship". P2 always fiddling with her hair and with her arms crossed
Dedication	1	PI "Ethics, companionship and dedication."
Punctuality	1	P3 "Ethics, working within the rules, commitment and punctuality".
Interpersonal relationships	1	P4 "Commitment, interpersonal relationships and loyalty".

Question 2: How do you rate the image that the Company (Banking Institution) has with the population of Goiânia? (very bad, bad, fair, good or excellent)

Category	Frequency	Verbalisation
Good	3	Pl,P2and P4 "Good"
Excellent	1	P3 "Excellent"

Question 3: Which other companies would be considered "competitors" of the bank?

Category	Frequency	Verbalisation
Banco do Brasil, Itaú, Bradesco	4	P1, P3 and P4 "Banco do Brasil, Itaú, Bradesco"

Question 4: How do you rate the bank's performance in relation to them?

Category	Frequency	Verbalisation
Service	3	PI "Service and fair rates"
Technology and Investment	1	P2
Fair rates	1	PI
More qualified and helpful staff	1	P3
Caring for the underprivileged community	1	P1 "Service and fair rates"

Question 7: In your opinion, what are the company's main strengths? A strength is something the organisation does well or a characteristic that gives it an important capability that contributes to its success. Try to name the top 3:

Category	Frequency	Verbalisation
Career plan	2	P3"Public credibility, career plan and salary."
A pioneer in housing	1	P2"Pioneer in housing, reliability and social benefits"

Question 8: A weakness is something that the organisation doesn't have or doesn't do very well and that compromises the company's success. In your opinion, try to highlight the company's main weaknesses (try to name at least the top 3):		
Category	Frequency	Verbalisation
Lack of technology	3	P4 "Lack of technology and virtual service"
Overload	2	Pl. "Overload, (...)"
Excessive standards	1	P3 "Overload and excessive standards within the company"
Virtual service	1	P4

Question 9: What kind of training could the company improve?		
Category	Frequency	Verbalisation
Training	4	Pl, P2, P3 and P4
Recognition	1	P2 "Sales training, integration of results and recognition".
Relationships between colleagues	1	Pl"Relationship training among co-workers to improve camaraderie, more training on the institution's products and services."
Companionship	1	P1

Question 10: What additional suggestions, comments, compliments or criticisms would you make of the company?
Pl. Praise: "Excellent organisational climate". Criticism: "To be seen more as a person, seeing your limits"; Suggestion: "To have a number of employees that matches the amount of work".
P2. Suggestion: "Benefits and better trained managers".
P3. Suggestion: "Employees should have a more active voice"; Criticism: "Too much work for too few people"; Praise: "Despite all this, he likes working for the company".
P4. Suggestion: "Implement virtual customer service" Criticism: "Improve the system and the measurement of targets"; Praise: "People management (transparent), support, environment".

Source: Lima; Ribeiro, Silva / May 2016.

Annex II

Averages of the Factors analysed at ECO - Banking Institution

Departments	Average Factor I	Average Factor II	Average Factor III	Average Factor IV	Average V Factor
Individual Service	3,0	2,4	3,0	3,3	3,4
Individual Support	2,9	2,7	3,4	3,2	3,5
Cashier service	3,3	2,7	3,1	3,4	3,7
Service/Housing Support	3,6	3,2	3,6	3,0	3,6
Final average	3,2	2,7	3,3	3,2	3,6
Evaluation	Regular	Negative	Regular	Regular	Regular

Source: Lima; Ribeiro, Silva / May 2016.

Annex III

Average Factor I

PERSONAL SERVICE				
Factor	Positive	Negative	Average	Evaluation

29

Factor I - Management and organisational support	None	2,3 (Q-13) Innovations made by employees in their work are accepted by the company. 2,5 (Q-04) Tasks that take longer to complete are guided to the end by the boss. (Q-9) In this company, questions are answered.	3,0	Regular
PERSONAL SERVICE SUPPORT				
Factor	Positive	Negative.	Average	Evaluation
Factor I - Management and organisational support	None	2,1 (Q -15) The boss values the employee's opinion. 2,3 (Q-16) In this company, employees have a say in changes. 2,4 (Q-04) The tasks that take the longest to complete are guided to the end by the boss. (Q-10) Here, tasks are planned. 2,7 (Q-02) The conflicts that occur in my work are resolved by the group itself. (Q-12) Changes in this company are planned. 2,8 (Q-03) The employee receives guidance from the supervisor (or boss) to carry out their tasks	2,9	Regular
CASHIER SERVICE				
Factor	Positive	Negative	Average	Evaluation
Factor I - Management and organisational support	None	2,0 (Q -16) In this company, employees have a say in changes. 2,3 (Q-15) The boss values the employee's opinion. 2,4 (Q - 08) Employees are informed about changes in the company. 2,6 (Q -13) Innovations made by employees in their work are accepted by the company. 2,8 (Q -12) Changes in this company are planned.	3,3	Regular
HOUSING SUPPORT				
Factor	Positive	Negative	Average	Evaluation
Factor I - Management and organisational support	None	2,3 (Q - 12) Changes in this company are planned. (Q - 16) In this company, employees have a say in changes	3,6	Regular

Source: Lima; Ribeiro, Silva / May 2016.

Annex IV

Average Factor II

PERSONAL SERVICE				
Factor	Positive	Negative	Average	Evaluation
Factor II - Reward	None	2,2 (Q-29) The rewards the employee receives are within their expectations. (Q-30) Work well done	2,7	Negative

Factor	Positive	Negative	Average	Evaluation
		is rewarded.		
		2,4		
		(Q-25) What employees earn depends on the tasks they do.		
		2,6		
		(Q-24) When employees do their job well, they are rewarded 2.8		
		(Q-28) This company values employee effort.		

PERSONAL SERVICE SUPPORT				
Factor	Positive	Negative	Average	Evaluation
Factor II - Reward	None	2,1 (Q - 25) What employees earn depends on the tasks they do.	2,7	Negative

CASHIER SERVICE				
Factor	Positive	Negative	Average	Evaluation
Factor II - Reward	None	2,2 (Q-29) The rewards the employee receives are within their expectations. (Q-30) Work well done is rewarded. 2,4 (Q-25) What employees earn depends on the tasks they do. 2,6 (Q-24) When employees do their job well, they are rewarded 2.8 (Q-28) This company values employee effort.	2,7	Negative

HOUSING CARE/SUPPORT				
Factor	Positive	Negative	Average	Evaluation
Factor II - Reward	None	2,3 (Q - 25) What employees earn depends on the tasks they do.	3,2	Regular

Source: Lima; Ribeiro, Silva / May 2016.

Annex V

Average Factor III

PERSONAL SERVICE				
Factor	Positive	Negative	Average	Evaluation
Factor III - Physical comfort	4.1 (Q40) The work area is clean.	2,2 (Q-36) In this company, the workplace is airy. 2,5 (Q-31) This company's employees have the necessary equipment to carry out their tasks. (Q-33) In this company, the disabled can move around easily.	3,0	Regular

PERSONAL SERVICE SUPPORT				
Factor	Positive	Negative	Average	Evaluation
Factor III - Physical comfort	4.1 (Q40) The work area is clean.	2,8 (Q - 33) The physical space in the work area is sufficient.	3,4	Regular

CASHIER SERVICE				
Factor	Positive	Negative	Average	Evaluation
Factor III - Physical comfort	None	2,2 (Q - 42) In this company, the physical posture of employees is appropriate to avoid damaging their	3,1	Regular

		health.		
		2,4		
		(Q-32) The work environment meets the physical needs of the worker.		
		2,6		
		(Q-33) In this company, the disabled can move around easily.		
		2,8		
		(Q-41) The work equipment is adequate to guarantee the employee's health at work.		
HOUSING SUPPORT				
Factor	Positive	Negative	Average	Evaluation
Factor III - Physical comfort	None	2,3 (Q - 25) In this company, the workplace is airy.	3,6	Regular

Source: Lima; Ribeiro, Silva / May 2016.

Annex VI

Average Factor IV

PERSONAL SERVICE				
Factor	Positive	Negative	Average	Evaluation
Factor IV - Control and pressure	None	4,0 (Q46) This company requires tasks to be done on time.	3,3	Regular
PERSONAL SERVICE SUPPORT				
Factor	Positive	Negative	Average	Evaluation
Factor IV- Control and pressure	2,4 (Q-44) There is too much control over employees here. 2,7 (Q - 45) In this company, everything is controlled.	4,0 (Q46) This company requires tasks to be done on time.	3,2	Regular
CASHIER SERVICE				
Factor	Positive	Negative	Average	Evaluation
Factor IV - Control and pressure	None	4,0 (Q46) This company requires tasks to be done on time.	3,3	Regular
HOUSING SUPPORT SERVICE				
Factor	Positive	Negative	Average	Evaluation
Factor IV - Control and pressure	2,0 (Q-48) Here, the boss uses company rules to punish employees. 2,3 (Q - 50) Here, the boss pressures you all the time	4,0 (Q46) This company requires tasks to be done on time.	3,0	Regular

Source: Lima; Ribeiro, Silva / May 2016.

Annex VII

Average V Factor

PERSONAL SERVICE				

Factor	Positive	Negative	Average	Evaluation
Factor V - Cohesion between colleagues	None	None	3,4	Regular
PERSONAL SERVICE SUPPORT				
Factor	Positive	Negative	Average	Evaluation
Factor V - Cohesion between colleagues	None	None	3,5	Regular
TELLER SUPPORT				
Factor	Positive	Negative	Average	Evaluation
Factor V - Cohesion between colleagues	4,2 (Q-54) Employees who make mistakes are helped by their colleagues	None	3,7	Regular
HOUSING CARE/SUPPORT				
Factor	Positive	Negative	Average	Evaluation
Factor V - Cohesion between colleagues	4.0 (Q-53) Relationships between people in this sector are friendly. 4.0 (Q - 55) Here, colleagues help a new employee with their difficulties.	None	3,6	Regular

Source: Lima; Ribeiro, Silva / May 2016.

Annex VIII

Average of the Factors analysed in ECO by Area

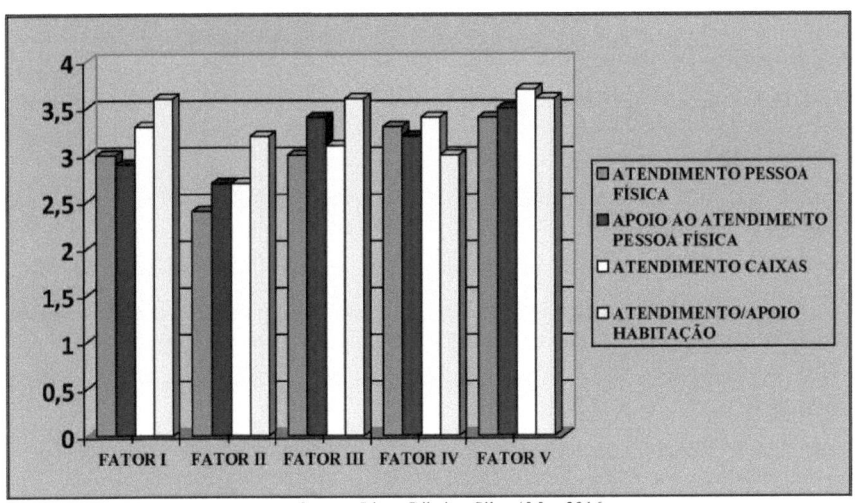

Source: Lima; Ribeiro, Silva / May 2016.

REFERENCES

BARDIN, L. Content analysis. Lisbon, Editions 70, 2002.

33

BENAGLIA, M. The influence of the work environment and lifestyle on workers' health. Available at: http://www.abepro.org.br/biblioteca/Acesso: 03 Jun 2016

BOCK, A.; FURTADO, O.; TEIXEIRA, M. Psicologia Fácil. São Paulo: Saraiva, 2012. p. 37-38/121/169.

CAPITÃO, C.G.; HELOANI, J. R. Mental health and work psychology. São Paulo em Perspectiva, 2003. v. 17, n. 2, p. 05/102-108.

CARVALHO, G.M; MORAES, R. D. Work overload and illness at the Manaus Industrial Estate. São Paulo em Perspectiva, v. 17, n. 2, p. 03/102-108, 2003.

CHIAVENATO, I. Managing people. 3.ed. São Paulo: Makron Books, 1997.

FLEURY, A. D.; MACÊDO, K. B.(organiser); LANCMAN, S.. et al. O diálogo que transforma: a clínica psicodinâmica do trabalho. Goiânia: Editora PUC Goiás, 2015. p. 95-132.

DEJOURS, C.: The madness of work: a study of the psychopathology of labour. São Paulo: Cortez Editora, 2005. p. 60-62/126-132/133-139.

EVANGELISTA, F. How the motivation of bank employees is important for the efficiency of the system. Available at: https://www.grancursospresencial.com.br. /Accessed on: 05 Jun 2016.

FREUD, S. The malaise of civilisation. Rio de Janeiro: Editora Psicanalítica Internacional. Imago, 1987 (complete works, v.21). p. 18/29-31.

HARTER, J.; WAGNER, R. 12 elements of excellent management. Rio de Janeiro: GMT editores Ltda, 2009. p. 87-88/196-199.

JACQUES, M. G. O nexo causal em saúde/doença mental no trabalho: uma demanda para a psicologia. Porto Alegre: Psicologia em Revista, 2007. v.19, p. 19.

JUNIOR, E. V. A.; SILVA, R. M; SILVA, N. L. C. NASCIMENTO, A. S.: Ergonomic study of a Financial Institution in the city of Guarabira - PB. Salvador - BA: ENEGEP, 2013. p. 04.

LANDIM, J. M. M.; BEZERRA, M. M. M.; ALVES, M. N. T.; M. M.: Workers' Mental Health in Brazil: Emerging Issues. Id on Line Revista Multidisciplinar e de Psicologia, January 2017, vol. 10, n. 33, Supl 2. p. 186-196. ISSN: 1981-1179

MAGALHÃES, A.C.; MELO, F.A.O.; REIS, P. N. C.; SOUZA, A.R.; SOUZA, B.R.
How Organisational Climate affects the level of occupational stress.

Available at: http://www.aedb.br/seget/arquivos/artigos13/9418550.pdf/ Accessed on: 08 Oct 2016.

MENDES, A.; RESENDE, S. Survival as a strategy to endure suffering in banking work. Available at: https://periodicos.ufsc.br/ Accessed on: 20 May 2016.

MENEZES, G.; DUTRA, R. Work overload and illness at the Manaus Industrial Estate. Psicologia em Revista, 2011. v. 17, n. 3, p. 465-482.

OLIVEIRA, D. et al. Organisational climate: a factor in job satisfaction and effective results in the organisation. SIMPÓSIO DE EXCELÊNCIA EM GESTÃO E TECNOLOGIA, v. 9, 2012. p. 02.

PIOVEZAN, C. K.; RUBINO, J. D.: Study of the organisational climate in a perfume and cosmetics retail company. Maringá Management: Revista de Ciências Empresariais, 2011, v.08, n° 01, p. 30.

RESENDE, S.; MENDES, A. Survival as a strategy to endure suffering in banking work. Revista Psicologia Organizações e Trabalho, 2004. v. 4, n°. 1, p. 151-175.

RODRIGUES, M. F. C.; MOLLICA, A. M. V.: Stress and quality of life in the work environment: a case study in a branch of the Brazilian banking system. Caderno Científico Fagoc de Graduação e Pós-graduação, 2016. v. 1, p. 38-45.

SIQUEIRA, M. Measures of organisational behaviour. São Paulo: Artmed Editora S.A, 2008. p. 34-36.

SILVA, N. Organisational diagnosis. In. BENDASSOLLI, P. F.; ANDRADE, J. E. B. (Orgs). Dictionary of work and organisational psychology. Casa do Psicólogo, 2014. 1ª Ed. p. 01-02/295 - 303.

SOUZA, J. As chefes avassaladoras. Osasco, SP: Novo Século Editora Ltda, 2009. p.183-184.

VASCOCELOS, A.; FARIA, J. H.: Mental health at work: contradictions and limits. Florianópolis - SC: Revista Psicologia Social, 2008. v. 20, p. 03/07-09.

VOLPE, R. The importance of training for work development. Psicologia Online, 2009. p. 01-08.

WEIL, P.; TOMPAKOW. The body speaks. Chap. 12: Practical Vocabulary. Petrópolis - RJ: Editora Vozes Ltda, 2009. 65th Ed. p. 169.

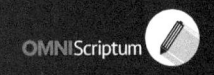

Printed by Books on Demand GmbH, Norderstedt / Germany